SUPER STRUCTURES

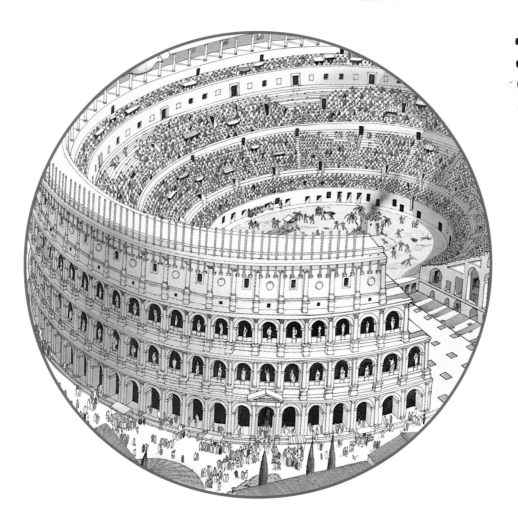

WITHDRAWN

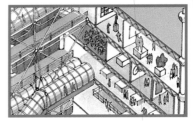

Author:

John Malam studied ancient history and archaeology at the University of Birmingham, after which he worked as an archaeologist at the Ironbridge Gorge Museum, Shropshire. He is now an author, specializing in information books for children. He lives in Cheshire with his wife, a book designer, and their two children.

Artist:

Mark Bergin was born in Hastings, England, in 1961. He studied at Eastbourne College of Art and has specialized in historical reconstructions, aviation, and maritime subjects since 1983. He has illustrated many books in the Fast Forward and prize-winning Inside Story series. He lives in Bexhill-on-Sea with his wife and three children.

Series creator:

David Salariya was born in Dundee, Scotland. He has illustrated a wide range of books and has created many new series of books for publishers in the UK and overseas. In 1989 he established The Salariya Book Company. He lives in Brighton with his wife, the illustrator Shirley Willis, and their son.

Editor:

Karen Barker Smith

Additional artists:

Nick Hewetson
John James
David Stewart
Gerald Wood

Created, designed, and produced by
THE SALARIYA BOOK COMPANY LTD
25 Marlborough Place, Brighton BN1 1UB

ISBN 0-531-11875-4 (Lib. Bdg.)
ISBN 0-531-16441-1 (Pbk.)

Published in America by Franklin Watts
Grolier Publishing Co., Inc.
90 Sherman Turnpike, Danbury, CT 06816

Visit Franklin Watts on the
Internet at: http://publishing.grolier.com

A CIP catalog record for this title is available from the Library of Congress.

Repro by Modern Age.

Printed in China

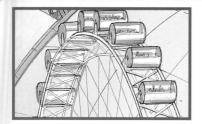

SUPER STRUCTURES

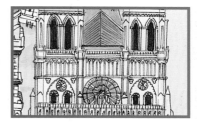

Written by

JOHN MALAM

Illustrated by

MARK BERGIN

Created and designed by

DAVID SALARIYA

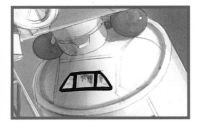

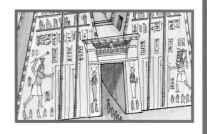

W
FRANKLIN WATTS
A Division of Grolier Publishing
NEW YORK • LONDON • HONG KONG • SYDNEY
DANBURY, CONNECTICUT

Contents

Stonehenge (left), in southern England, is Europe's greatest prehistoric structure, built around 2550 B.C. It was used for religious ceremonies. Large stones, called sarsens, were dragged for 19 mi (30 km) to the site. Smaller stones, called bluestones, were moved by water and then over land from south Wales, 150 mi (240 km) away.

Some of the world's first structures were built from mud. It was shaped into small rectangular blocks that were left to bake hard in the sun. In ancient Egypt and Mesopotamia, mud bricks were used for buildings ranging from houses (left) to high towers called ziggurats. They were also used by the civilizations of South America.

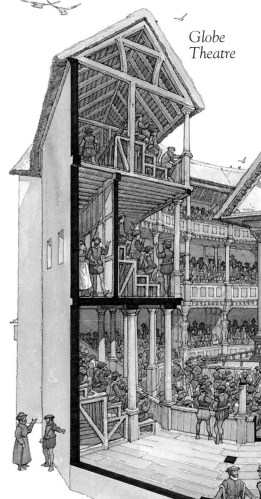

Globe Theatre

Building Materials

The world's structures are made from an incredible variety of building materials. The remains of shelters made in eastern Europe during the last Ice Age are among the oldest in the world. At that time, about 20,000 years ago, bones and tusks from woolly mammoths were stood on end and covered with skins and branches to make simple huts. Later, people learned how to work with timber, stone, and mud. These basic building materials were used all over the world, as they still are today. In modern times, new materials have replaced many of the older, traditional ones. In industrialized countries, timber was overtaken by brick, which in turn has been replaced by metal, concrete, glass, and plastic. But for some structures, the old materials are still the best, such as the use of reeds in thatching roofs.

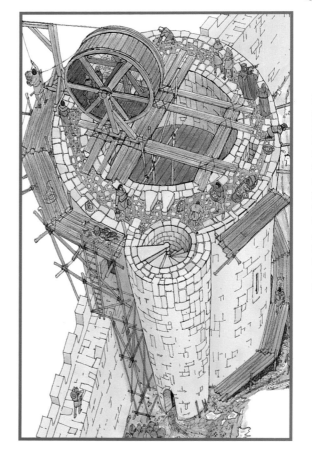

In the Middle Ages, stone castles were built in Europe and North Africa. Many towns were also surrounded with stone walls for protection. Stone was quarried and shaped by hand. At the construction site, masons lifted stone with machinery (left) and stuck it together with mortar.

Timber is a hard, long-lasting material with great strength. It was widely used in Europe until the 1600s, when brick buildings became more common. Bricks were safer to use because they did not burn.

Timber-framed buildings were most often made from oak, put together like a giant jigsaw. Each piece of timber was cut by hand and assembly instructions, called carpenter's marks, were scratched onto them. At the construction site, the marks were matched together and the timbers slotted into place. For extra strength, timbers were held together with wooden pegs called tree-nails, hammered into drilled holes.

Plaster is spread like paste onto walls and ceilings. It sets hard and can then be painted. Plaster was traditionally made from burnt limestone mixed with sand, water, and animal hair.

Thatch is a thick covering of reeds, rushes, or straw. A thatched roof provides good insulation, keeping a building warm and dry. The best thatch can last up to 80 years before being renewed.

The Pompidou Center (below) in Paris, France, was opened in 1977. It is a huge building made up of exhibition galleries, a concert hall, theater, library, and restaurants. It is made from gigantic steel beams and supports, painted in bright colors. The outside is covered in huge metal pipes and ducts housing the Center's air conditioning, water supply, electrical cables, and other vital services. Usually these would be out of sight inside the structure, but the architects wanted people to see how the building worked, so they made it "inside out." There was a practical reason for putting its insides on show — when something needs repairing, it is easy to get at.

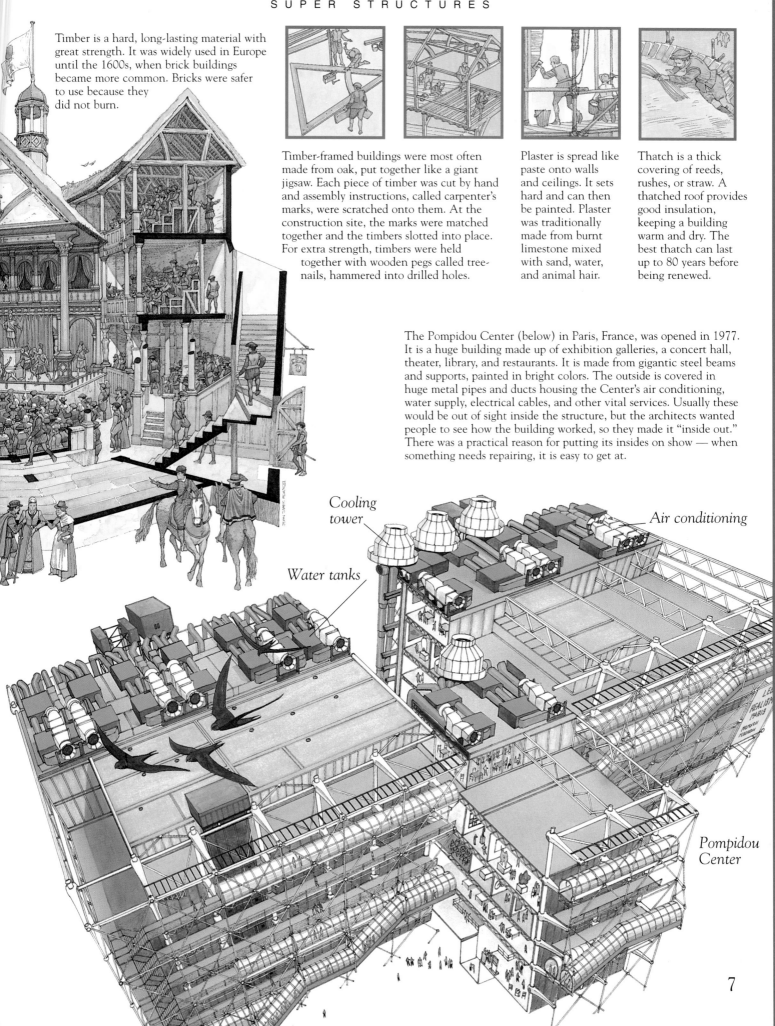

Cooling tower

Air conditioning

Water tanks

Pompidou Center

World-Famous Structures

S ome of the world's most fantastic structures are thousands of years old; others were built more recently. They are splendid examples of the skills of architects and builders.

Eiffel Tower

The Great Pyramid

The Great Pyramid at Giza, Egypt, was built about 2550 B.C. Around 20,000 laborers spent 23 years on its construction, cutting and moving 2.3 million blocks of limestone into place. It was 482 ft (147 m) high and was the world's tallest structure for over 4,000 years.

Built in 1889, the Eiffel Tower is a symbol of Paris, France. Made from 18,000 pieces of iron held together by 2.5 million rivets, it rises to a height of 984 ft (300 m). It was the world's tallest building until 1929.

Temple of Ramesses II

Colosseum

A stave church

St. Basil's Cathedral

Parthenon

The temple of pharaoh Ramesses II at Abu Simbel, Egypt, was carved from solid rock about 2165 B.C. At the front are four huge statues of the king, each about 72 ft (22 m) high.

The Parthenon overlooks Athens in Greece and was built between 447 and 438 B.C. Apart from the roof timbers, the whole building was made from 230,000 tons of marble.

Stave churches were built in Scandinavia between A.D. 1000 and 1100. They were named after the short upright timber posts, or staves, from which they were constructed.

The Colosseum in Rome was completed about A.D. 70. It was an open-air arena, with seats for up to 80,000 spectators. It was made from concrete and blocks of volcanic limestone called travertine.

St. Basil's Cathedral is in Moscow, Russia. It was built between 1555 and 1561 and consists of eight chapels grouped around a central tower.

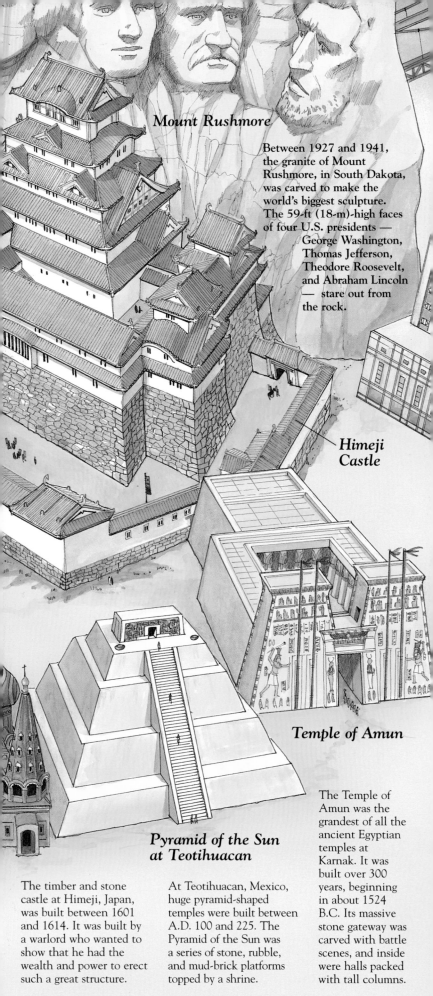

Mount Rushmore

Between 1927 and 1941, the granite of Mount Rushmore, in South Dakota, was carved to make the world's biggest sculpture. The 59-ft (18-m)-high faces of four U.S. presidents — George Washington, Thomas Jefferson, Theodore Roosevelt, and Abraham Lincoln — stare out from the rock.

Himeji Castle

Temple of Amun

Pyramid of the Sun at Teotihuacan

The timber and stone castle at Himeji, Japan, was built between 1601 and 1614. It was built by a warlord who wanted to show that he had the wealth and power to erect such a great structure.

At Teotihuacan, Mexico, huge pyramid-shaped temples were built between A.D. 100 and 225. The Pyramid of the Sun was a series of stone, rubble, and mud-brick platforms topped by a shrine.

The Temple of Amun was the grandest of all the ancient Egyptian temples at Karnak. It was built over 300 years, beginning in about 1524 B.C. Its massive stone gateway was carved with battle scenes, and inside were halls packed with tall columns.

9

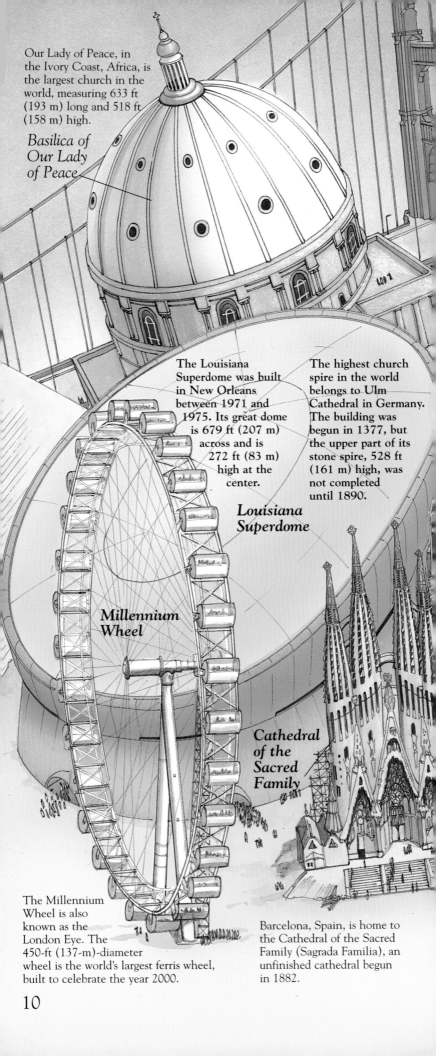

Our Lady of Peace, in the Ivory Coast, Africa, is the largest church in the world, measuring 633 ft (193 m) long and 518 ft (158 m) high.

Basilica of Our Lady of Peace

The Louisiana Superdome was built in New Orleans between 1971 and 1975. Its great dome is 679 ft (207 m) across and is 272 ft (83 m) high at the center.

The highest church spire in the world belongs to Ulm Cathedral in Germany. The building was begun in 1377, but the upper part of its stone spire, 528 ft (161 m) high, was not completed until 1890.

Louisiana Superdome

Millennium Wheel

Cathedral of the Sacred Family

The Millennium Wheel is also known as the London Eye. The 450-ft (137-m)-diameter wheel is the world's largest ferris wheel, built to celebrate the year 2000.

Barcelona, Spain, is home to the Cathedral of the Sacred Family (Sagrada Familia), an unfinished cathedral begun in 1882.

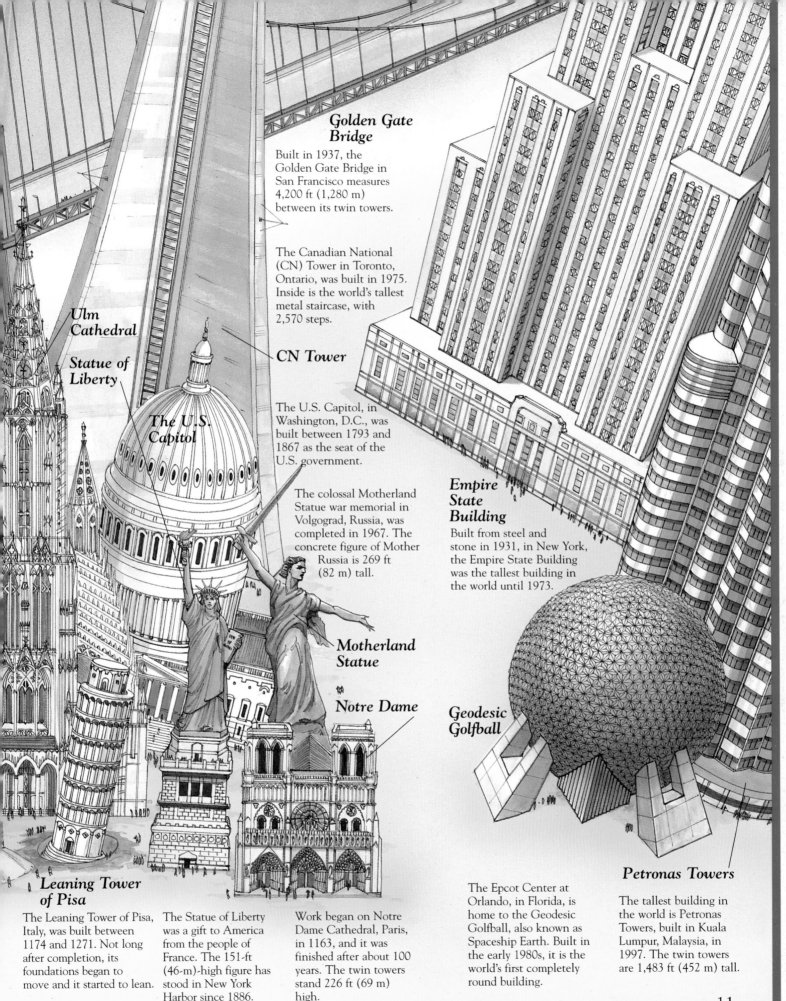

Golden Gate Bridge

Built in 1937, the Golden Gate Bridge in San Francisco measures 4,200 ft (1,280 m) between its twin towers.

The Canadian National (CN) Tower in Toronto, Ontario, was built in 1975. Inside is the world's tallest metal staircase, with 2,570 steps.

CN Tower

The U.S. Capitol, in Washington, D.C., was built between 1793 and 1867 as the seat of the U.S. government.

The colossal Motherland Statue war memorial in Volgograd, Russia, was completed in 1967. The concrete figure of Mother Russia is 269 ft (82 m) tall.

Ulm Cathedral

Statue of Liberty

The U.S. Capitol

Empire State Building

Built from steel and stone in 1931, in New York, the Empire State Building was the tallest building in the world until 1973.

Motherland Statue

Notre Dame

Geodesic Golfball

Leaning Tower of Pisa

The Leaning Tower of Pisa, Italy, was built between 1174 and 1271. Not long after completion, its foundations began to move and it started to lean.

The Statue of Liberty was a gift to America from the people of France. The 151-ft (46-m)-high figure has stood in New York Harbor since 1886.

Work began on Notre Dame Cathedral, Paris, in 1163, and it was finished after about 100 years. The twin towers stand 226 ft (69 m) high.

The Epcot Center at Orlando, in Florida, is home to the Geodesic Golfball, also known as Spaceship Earth. Built in the early 1980s, it is the world's first completely round building.

Petronas Towers

The tallest building in the world is Petronas Towers, built in Kuala Lumpur, Malaysia, in 1997. The twin towers are 1,483 ft (452 m) tall.

Power Building

A grand structure is a sign of the power and wealth of those who built it. In ancient times it also signified the ability of a leader to control a large workforce. Impressive, large-scale monuments were built in both ancient Egypt and Mexico. Although 3,000 years and thousands of miles separated the two civilizations, both created pyramid-shaped structures. While Egyptian pyramids were built as tombs, Aztec pyramids had a more sinister use — they were manmade mountains on which people were sacrificed to the gods. Castles are another type of power building, built to resist attack and protect the people inside them.

The Aztec capital in Mexico was Tenochtitlan, in the middle of which stood the Great Temple. This pyramid-shaped structure was the religious center of the Aztec empire. A double flight of steps led to the top, upon which were two shrines. The temple was extended many times, and by the early 1500s it was about 98 ft (30 m) high.

In Egypt about 4,500 years ago, a group of stone pyramids was built at Giza. The three largest were tombs for the pharaohs Khufu, Khafre, and Menkaure, while smaller ones were built for their queens. Pyramids were monumental structures, built to show the power of the royalty who had them erected. They were meant to stand forever.

The two shrines on top of the Great Temple were for the gods Huitzilopochtli (wee-tsee-lo-poch-tlee) and Tlaloc (tla-lok). They were two of the Aztecs' most important gods. To please them and give thanks, the gods were offered human sacrifices. Victims were stretched over an altar stone in front of the shrines, and a priest cut out their hearts with a sharp stone knife.

Shrine for Tlaloc, god of rain

Great Temple (Templo Mayor) of the Aztecs

Each staircase had 113 steps.

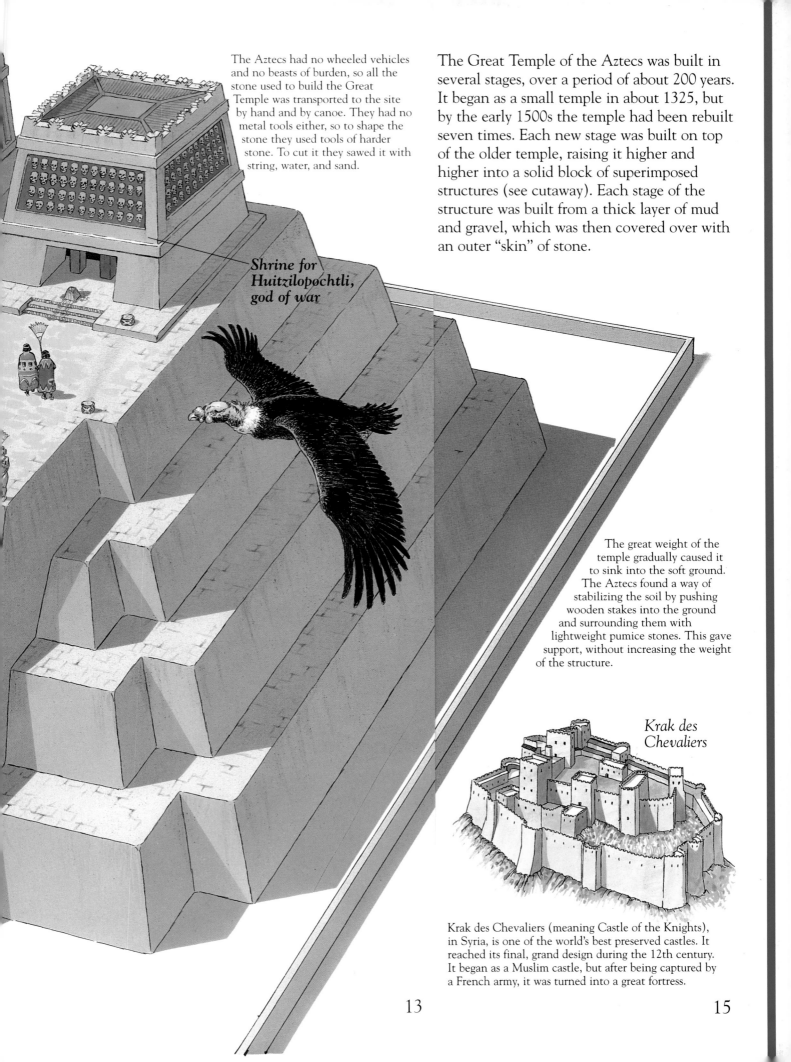

The Aztecs had no wheeled vehicles and no beasts of burden, so all the stone used to build the Great Temple was transported to the site by hand and by canoe. They had no metal tools either, so to shape the stone they used tools of harder stone. To cut it they sawed it with string, water, and sand.

The Great Temple of the Aztecs was built in several stages, over a period of about 200 years. It began as a small temple in about 1325, but by the early 1500s the temple had been rebuilt seven times. Each new stage was built on top of the older temple, raising it higher and higher into a solid block of superimposed structures (see cutaway). Each stage of the structure was built from a thick layer of mud and gravel, which was then covered over with an outer "skin" of stone.

Shrine for Huitzilopochtli, god of war

The great weight of the temple gradually caused it to sink into the soft ground. The Aztecs found a way of stabilizing the soil by pushing wooden stakes into the ground and surrounding them with lightweight pumice stones. This gave support, without increasing the weight of the structure.

Krak des Chevaliers

Krak des Chevaliers (meaning Castle of the Knights), in Syria, is one of the world's best preserved castles. It reached its final, grand design during the 12th century. It began as a Muslim castle, but after being captured by a French army, it was turned into a great fortress.

The Parthenon was named after Athena Parthenos, the patron goddess of Athens. Inside the temple stood a giant statue of her, 39 ft (12 m) high. Around the outside edge of the roof, sculptors carved a frieze showing scenes from Greek mythology, which was then painted in bright colors.

Parthenon

In the 4th century A.D., the statue of Athena was removed and the building was converted into a Christian church. It became a mosque in 1460 and when, in 1687, it was being used as a gunpowder store, it was blown up. Today, it is slowly being put back together again.

The Parthenon, Athens

The Parthenon is the largest temple on the Acropolis, the hill that rises above the city of Athens, Greece. The temple was built almost entirely from white marble, quarried at Mount Pentelicon 8 mi (13 km) away. It took a full day to transport stone from the quarry to the building site, and the heaviest blocks, weighing 10 tons each, needed a team of 30 donkeys to shift them. Timber was used for its doors and roof supports. More than 230,000 tons of marble was used, and it took nine years to complete. It was a great feat of engineering and design, and when it was finished, in 438 B.C., the Parthenon was the crowning glory of Athens.

Each monumental column was made up of ten or more marble blocks. Once in place, the bosses were cut off and vertical channels, or flutes, were carved from top to bottom.

The fine carving, called dressing, was done at the stonemasons' workshops on site. Stone handles, called bosses, were left on the blocks. This allowed ropes to be tied to them so that cranes could lift them into position.

Stonemasons used iron chisels, saws, drills, and hammers (right). Mortar was not used to join the blocks together. Instead, they were pinned together with iron clamps set into lead.

Bosses

The Colosseum, Rome

The Colosseum was a vast open-air structure, built by the Romans. It was used to stage gladiator contests and wild beast hunts. This towering structure, 170 ft (52 m) high, was a marvel of engineering. To build it in just eight years, it has been calculated that a cartload of stone arrived there every seven minutes, 12 hours a day. But the real secret of its construction was in the use of concrete. This lightweight but very strong material, invented by the Romans, supported the huge weight of the building.

Cranes

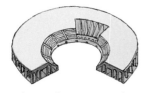

Work began in the early A.D. 70s, when a lake was drained to make way for the new building.

A layer of concrete and stone 43 ft (13 m) deep was made as the foundation for the oval-shaped Colosseum.

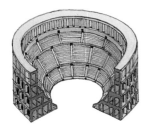

Three tiers of seats were built over a network of concrete vaults and passages.

The building was opened in A.D. 80. It had seats for between 50,000 and 80,000 spectators.

Cranes were used to lift the heavy stone into place. Lighter building materials, such as brick and concrete, were used to make the upper levels. Around the very top were 240 wooden masts, which supported an awning — a giant sheet pulled across the arena to shade it from the sun.

Eighty arches around the base of the building gave access to the spectators' seats. The Roman emperor and senators sat on marble seats in the first tier. Men sat in the first and second tiers while women sat in the top tier. Slaves could stand behind them.

Masts

Entrance arch

Building for Worship

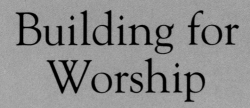

Religion has always had a great influence on architecture. Temples from the time of ancient Egypt, Greece, and Rome still exist — they were built to last, using the best methods and materials of the day. Great cathedrals from the Middle Ages still dominate the old towns of Europe, while magnificent mosques are the focus of worship in Islamic countries. Modern building materials and imaginative designs are used to create today's grand buildings for worship. If cared for by future generations, they too might still be standing in 1,000 years time.

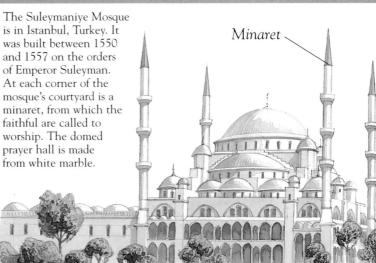

The Suleymaniye Mosque is in Istanbul, Turkey. It was built between 1550 and 1557 on the orders of Emperor Suleyman. At each corner of the mosque's courtyard is a minaret, from which the faithful are called to worship. The domed prayer hall is made from white marble.

Minaret

Some European churches built in the Middle Ages had labyrinth mosaics on their floors. People danced towards the middle, which symbolized Jerusalem, the center of the Christian world. The labyrinth at Chartres Cathedral, France, was made of 365 stones — one for every day of the year.

Framework for wheel (or rose) window

Towering above the houses of Chartres, France, is its great cathedral — a masterpiece of medieval building. Work began in 1194 and went on for 400 years.
To save on transport costs, local people volunteered to drag stone from the quarry 5 mi (8 km) away. At the building site the stone was shaped by master masons, who followed the architects' drawings. Laborers used cranes and hoists to lift the blocks of stone into place, and mortar was used to join the blocks together.

Not long after Christianity reached Norway, about 1,000 years ago, timber churches were built in a unique style. Short upright posts, called staves, were set into horizontal wall beams, making a solid structure built entirely from timber. Even the roof tiles were made from wood. Today, 29 of these stave-built churches survive, of which the largest and most ornate is Borgund church, built about 1150. On its roof are dragons' heads, carved in a Viking style.

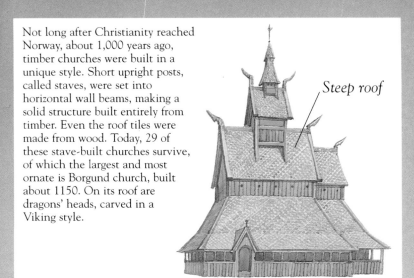

Steep roof

Hoist to raise stone

Timber scaffolding

Spire built
between 1507
and 1514

Pointed
pinnacle

Wheel (or rose) window,
containing stained glass

Pointed
window

20

Spire built between 1145 and 1170

Stone figures from Chartres Cathedral

More than 10,000 figures and gargoyles decorate the inside and outside of Chartres Cathedral. Stone was carved to create the statues of saints and apostles on the outside of the building (above). Wood and glass were used for the figures inside. Chartres is famous for its 160 stained-glass windows. Altogether the windows contain about 22,002 ft² (2,044 m²) of colored glass, showing not only religious scenes, but pictures of the craftsmen who built the cathedral.

A new style of church architecture developed in Constantinople (present-day Istanbul), Turkey, in the 6th century A.D. Churches in this Byzantine style have spectacular domes.

The style spread to eastern Europe and was used in the building of St. Basil's Cathedral (1555–61) in Moscow, Russia.

St. Basil's Cathedral

Dome, or cupola

Building work for Brazil's newest capital city, Brasilia, began in the mid-1950s. Brazilian architect Oscar Niemeyer created the city's cathedral, completed in 1970. The circular structure was built from glass, steel, and concrete.

The concrete buttresses swoop upward into a crown, representing the crown of thorns worn by Christ.

Brasilia Cathedral

Timber-framed domestic building

Chartres Cathedral was built in a style of architecture called Gothic, which began in France in the late 1100s. Gothic buildings have a distinctive pointed look about them. The tops of windows and arches are pointed, and pointed pinnacles and spires soar up to heaven. Gothic was especially popular for religious buildings, but it was rarely used for domestic structures, such as houses, which were built from cheaper building materials in a plainer style.

Akashi-Kaikyo Bridge

Golden Gate Bridge

Pont de Normandie

The Akashi-Kaikyo Bridge, Japan, is the world's longest suspension bridge. The center span is 6,529 ft (1,990 m) long.

Sydney Harbour Bridge

Bridges and Tunnels

Building bridges and tunnels is a great challenge, not only to architects and civil engineers, but also to the machines and building materials they use. For example, machines such as tunnel borers have to be specially built to cut their way through solid rock, and incredibly strong steel cables have to be made to hold up the world's newest bridges.

In ancient Egyptian underground tombs, a passage was tunneled into rock, at the end of which were chambers where the body was placed and surrounded by goods for the afterlife.

Egyptian tomb

Sydney Harbour Bridge, Australia, was built between 1924 and 1932. It is a steel arch bridge with a span of 1,650 ft (503 m) between its stone towers, called pylons.

The Seikan Tunnel is the world's longest rail tunnel at 34 mi (54 km). Completed in 1988, it cuts through rock at an average depth of 299 ft (91 m) below the seabed, to link the two main islands of Japan.

Seikan Tunnel

le Shuttle

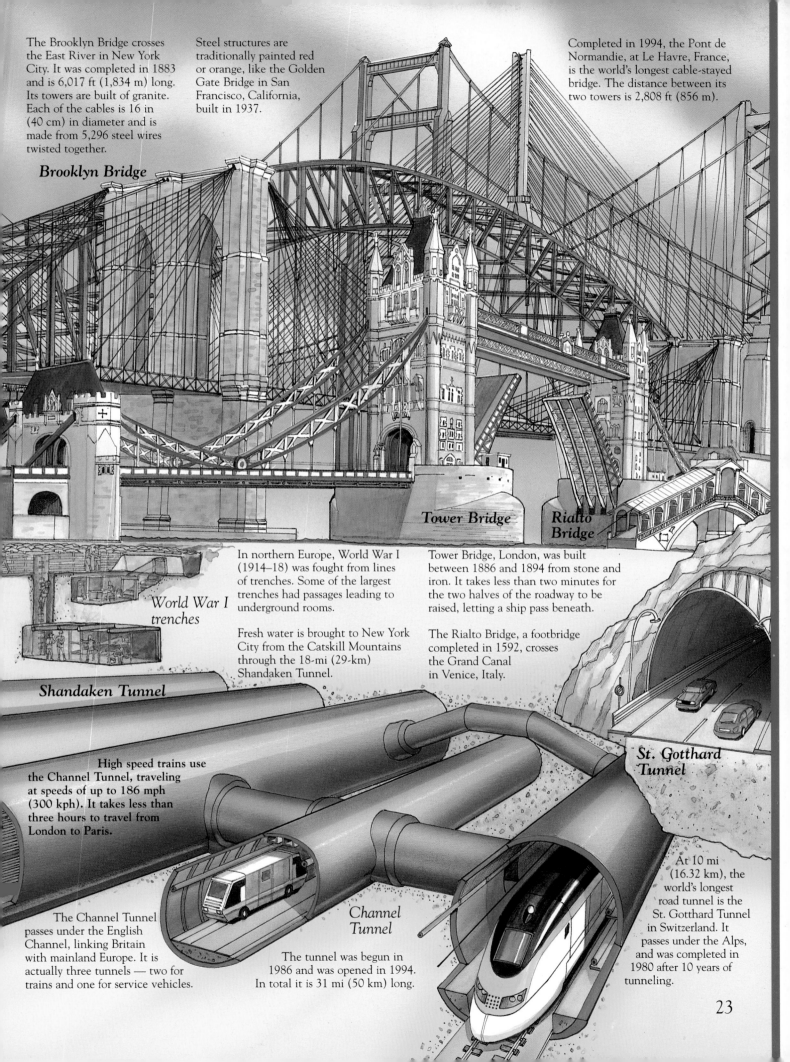

The Brooklyn Bridge crosses the East River in New York City. It was completed in 1883 and is 6,017 ft (1,834 m) long. Its towers are built of granite. Each of the cables is 16 in (40 cm) in diameter and is made from 5,296 steel wires twisted together.

Brooklyn Bridge

Steel structures are traditionally painted red or orange, like the Golden Gate Bridge in San Francisco, California, built in 1937.

Completed in 1994, the Pont de Normandie, at Le Havre, France, is the world's longest cable-stayed bridge. The distance between its two towers is 2,808 ft (856 m).

Tower Bridge

Rialto Bridge

World War I trenches

In northern Europe, World War I (1914–18) was fought from lines of trenches. Some of the largest trenches had passages leading to underground rooms.

Fresh water is brought to New York City from the Catskill Mountains through the 18-mi (29-km) Shandaken Tunnel.

Tower Bridge, London, was built between 1886 and 1894 from stone and iron. It takes less than two minutes for the two halves of the roadway to be raised, letting a ship pass beneath.

The Rialto Bridge, a footbridge completed in 1592, crosses the Grand Canal in Venice, Italy.

Shandaken Tunnel

St. Gotthard Tunnel

High speed trains use the Channel Tunnel, traveling at speeds of up to 186 mph (300 kph). It takes less than three hours to travel from London to Paris.

The Channel Tunnel passes under the English Channel, linking Britain with mainland Europe. It is actually three tunnels — two for trains and one for service vehicles.

Channel Tunnel

The tunnel was begun in 1986 and was opened in 1994. In total it is 31 mi (50 km) long.

At 10 mi (16.32 km), the world's longest road tunnel is the St. Gotthard Tunnel in Switzerland. It passes under the Alps, and was completed in 1980 after 10 years of tunneling.

23

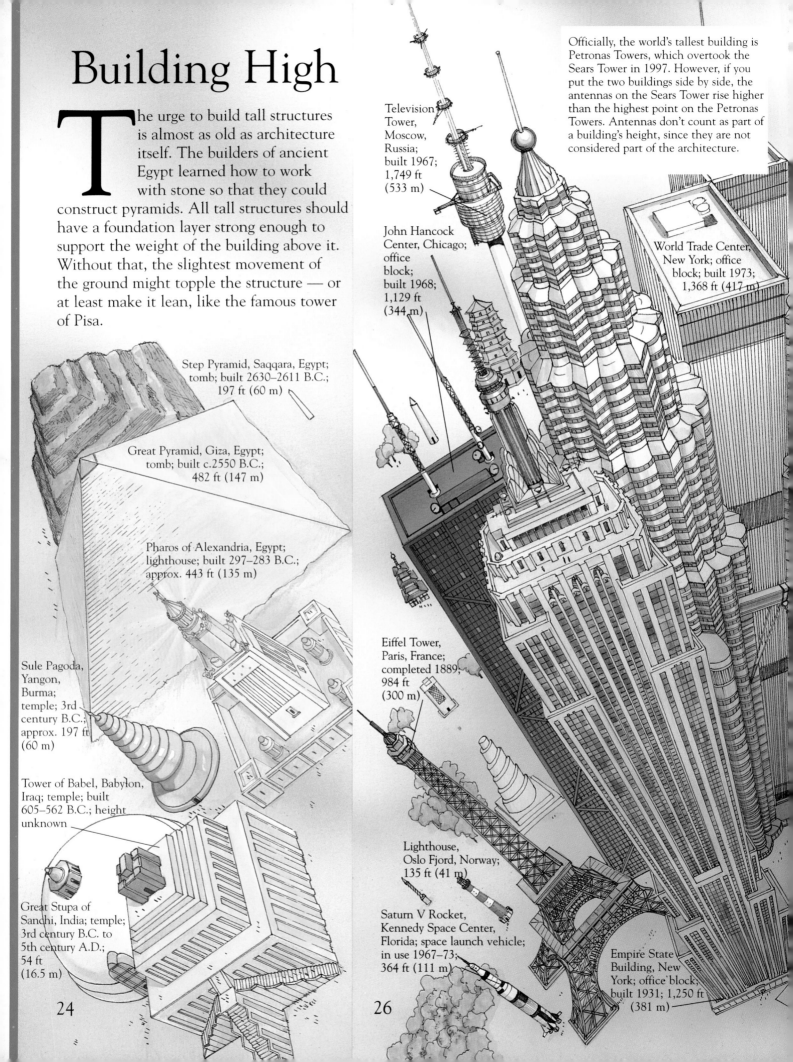

Building High

The urge to build tall structures is almost as old as architecture itself. The builders of ancient Egypt learned how to work with stone so that they could construct pyramids. All tall structures should have a foundation layer strong enough to support the weight of the building above it. Without that, the slightest movement of the ground might topple the structure — or at least make it lean, like the famous tower of Pisa.

Step Pyramid, Saqqara, Egypt; tomb; built 2630–2611 B.C.; 197 ft (60 m)

Great Pyramid, Giza, Egypt; tomb; built c.2550 B.C.; 482 ft (147 m)

Pharos of Alexandria, Egypt; lighthouse; built 297–283 B.C.; approx. 443 ft (135 m)

Sule Pagoda, Yangon, Burma; temple; 3rd century B.C.; approx. 197 ft (60 m)

Tower of Babel, Babylon, Iraq; temple; built 605–562 B.C.; height unknown

Great Stupa of Sanchi, India; temple; 3rd century B.C. to 5th century A.D.; 54 ft (16.5 m)

24

Television Tower, Moscow, Russia; built 1967; 1,749 ft (533 m)

John Hancock Center, Chicago; office block; built 1968; 1,129 ft (344 m)

Officially, the world's tallest building is Petronas Towers, which overtook the Sears Tower in 1997. However, if you put the two buildings side by side, the antennas on the Sears Tower rise higher than the highest point on the Petronas Towers. Antennas don't count as part of a building's height, since they are not considered part of the architecture.

World Trade Center, New York; office block; built 1973; 1,368 ft (417 m)

Eiffel Tower, Paris, France; completed 1889; 984 ft (300 m)

Lighthouse, Oslo Fjord, Norway; 135 ft (41 m)

Saturn V Rocket, Kennedy Space Center, Florida; space launch vehicle; in use 1967–73; 364 ft (111 m)

Empire State Building, New York; office block; built 1931; 1,250 ft (381 m)

26

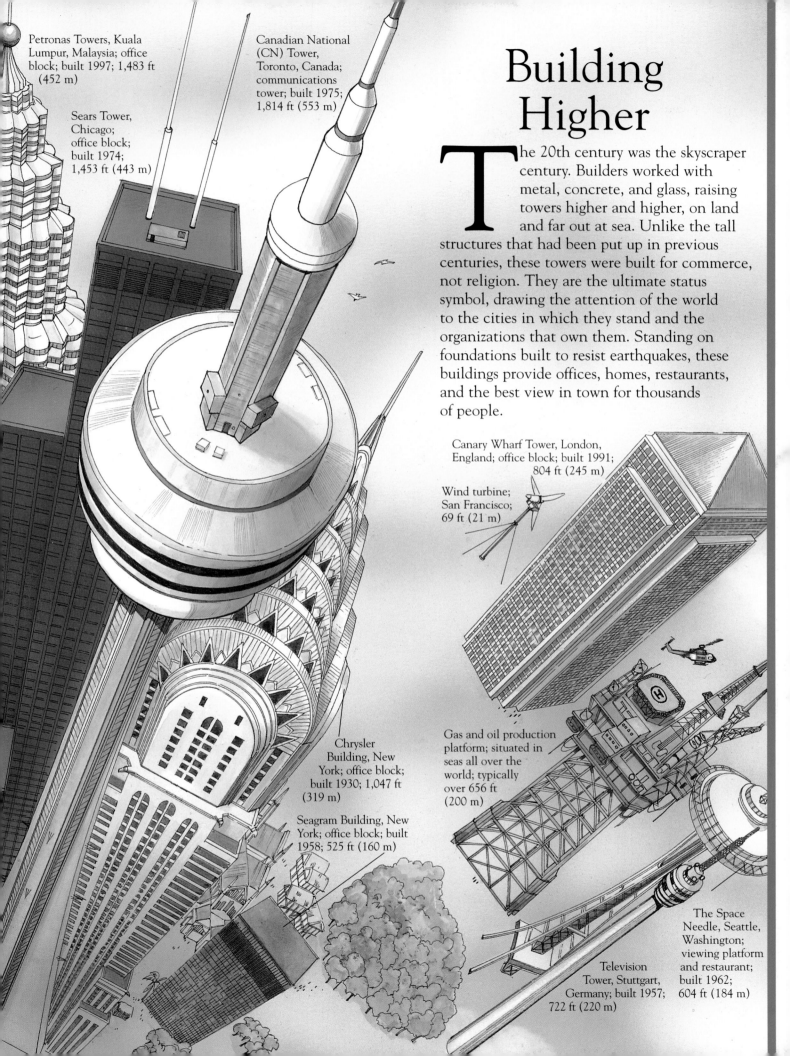

Petronas Towers, Kuala Lumpur, Malaysia; office block; built 1997; 1,483 ft (452 m)

Sears Tower, Chicago; office block; built 1974; 1,453 ft (443 m)

Canadian National (CN) Tower, Toronto, Canada; communications tower; built 1975; 1,814 ft (553 m)

Building Higher

The 20th century was the skyscraper century. Builders worked with metal, concrete, and glass, raising towers higher and higher, on land and far out at sea. Unlike the tall structures that had been put up in previous centuries, these towers were built for commerce, not religion. They are the ultimate status symbol, drawing the attention of the world to the cities in which they stand and the organizations that own them. Standing on foundations built to resist earthquakes, these buildings provide offices, homes, restaurants, and the best view in town for thousands of people.

Canary Wharf Tower, London, England; office block; built 1991; 804 ft (245 m)

Wind turbine; San Francisco; 69 ft (21 m)

Chrysler Building, New York; office block; built 1930; 1,047 ft (319 m)

Seagram Building, New York; office block; built 1958; 525 ft (160 m)

Gas and oil production platform; situated in seas all over the world; typically over 656 ft (200 m)

The Space Needle, Seattle, Washington; viewing platform and restaurant; built 1962; 604 ft (184 m)

Television Tower, Stuttgart, Germany; built 1957; 722 ft (220 m)

Structures in Space

The biggest engineering project ever undertaken is now in progress — the building of the International Space Station (ISS). Sixteen nations have joined forces to work on the project. The first parts of the ISS were launched by Russia and the United States in 1998. It will take more than 40 spaceflights over five years to transport every component of the massive structure. Once complete, the ISS will have an international crew of seven astronauts orbiting the Earth at an altitude of 220 mi (354 km). They will spend up to six months at a time onboard the station, conducting experiments in its six laboratories. The ISS will be an engineering, scientific, and technological marvel, signaling a new era in human space exploration for the 21st century.

The International Space Station is one small part in a long-term mission to build a space base on the moon. Humans first visited the moon in 1969. Five more visits were made after that date, the last in 1972. A moon base will require an enormous amount of planning and international cooperation. When it is built it may look something like this artist's impression (below).

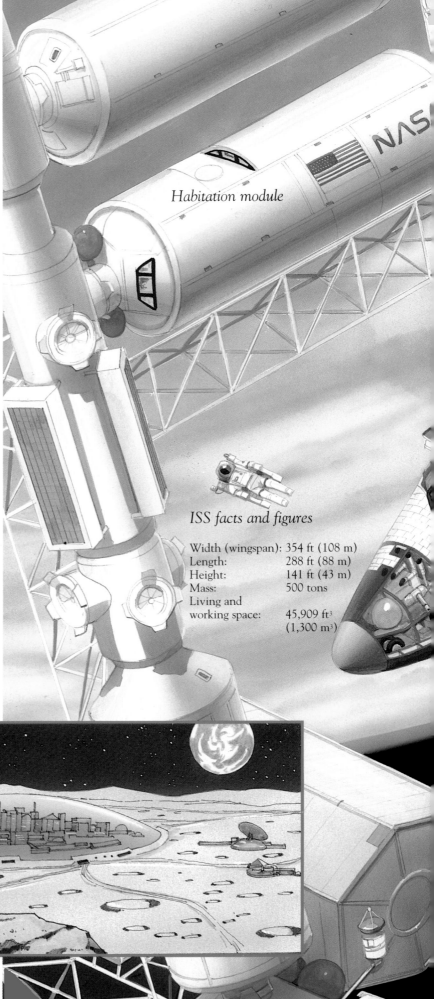

Habitation module

ISS facts and figures

Width (wingspan): 354 ft (108 m)
Length: 288 ft (88 m)
Height: 141 ft (43 m)
Mass: 500 tons
Living and
working space: 45,909 ft³
                 (1,300 m³)

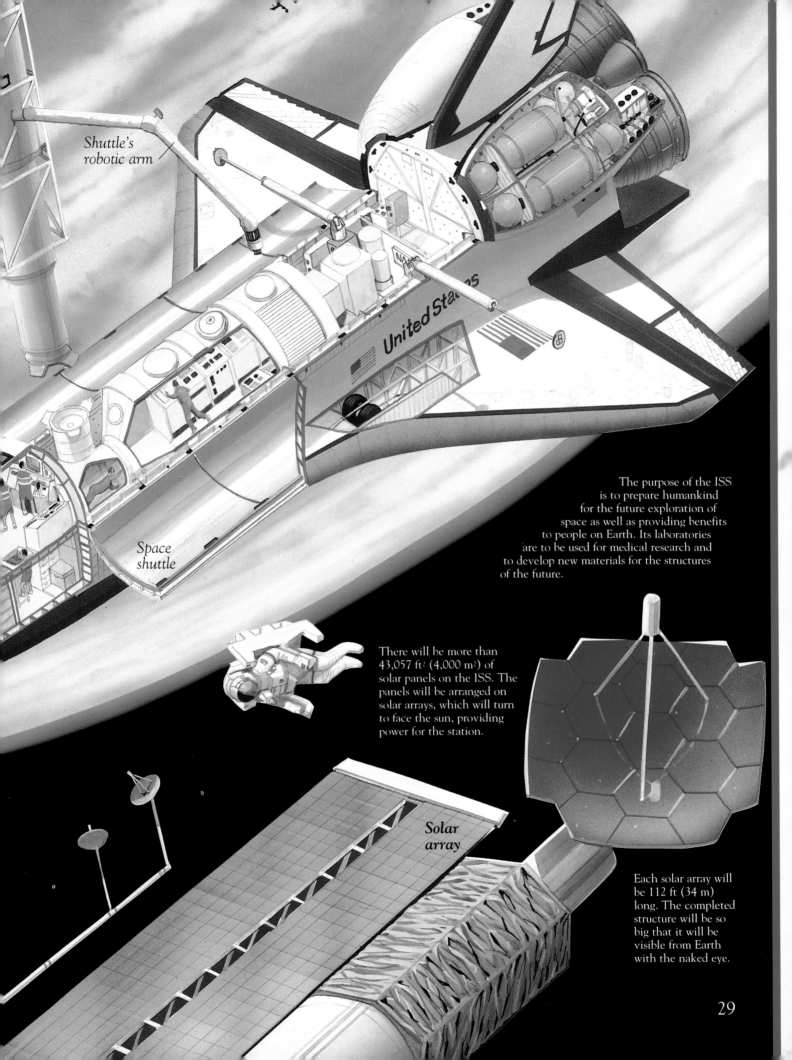

Shuttle's robotic arm

Space shuttle

The purpose of the ISS is to prepare humankind for the future exploration of space as well as providing benefits to people on Earth. Its laboratories are to be used for medical research and to develop new materials for the structures of the future.

There will be more than 43,057 ft² (4,000 m²) of solar panels on the ISS. The panels will be arranged on solar arrays, which will turn to face the sun, providing power for the station.

Solar array

Each solar array will be 112 ft (34 m) long. The completed structure will be so big that it will be visible from Earth with the naked eye.

29

Glossary

Architect
A person who designs and plans buildings.

Boss
A knob carved on a block of stone used as a handle to lift it with. Also, a decorative shape on an arched ceiling, such as inside a cathedral. From the French *bosse*, meaning lump or knob.

Carpenter's marks
Marks made on timbers that act as guides to how the pieces should be joined together.

Concrete
A mixture of water, sand, and cement that sets hard.

Cupola
A cup-shaped roof.

Dome
Another name for a cupola. It comes from the Italian word *duomo*, meaning cathedral.

Flute
A vertical channel carved into a stone column.

Gargoyle
A water-spout fed by water draining from a roof, carved as a grotesque creature. From the Latin *gurges*, meaning whirlpool.

Labyrinth
A maze-like pattern seen on the floors of European cathedrals and churches during the Middle Ages.

Limestone
A type of soft rock.

Marble
A type of hard rock.

Minaret
A tall, slender tower at a mosque from which a muezzin (a Muslim crier) calls the faithful to prayer five times a day.

Mortar
A mixture of water, sand, and lime used to join bricks and stones.

Mosque
A Muslim house of worship.

Mud brick
A shaped-block, usually rectangular, made from mud mixed with straw and baked hard by the sun.

Pinnacle
A small turret often built on European cathedrals and churches during the Middle Ages.

Plaster
A mixture used for coating the inside and outside of walls, traditionally made of lime, sand, and sometimes hair.

Pumice
A light-colored volcanic rock full of air pockets.

Rivet
A metal bolt used to fasten materials together, particularly metal.

Rose window
A wheel-shaped window used in European cathedrals and churches during the Middle Ages.

Sarsen
A type of hard stone.

Sculptor
A person who works with stone, making statues and decorative details.

Skyscraper
An extremely tall building.

Spire
The tapering tip of a tower, most commonly found on churches and cathedrals.

Stained glass
Colored glass used in decorative windows.

Stave
A short wooden post.

Steeple
A tower that has a spire.

Stonemason
A person who works with stone, cutting it into blocks.

Thatch
A roof-covering of reeds, rushes, or straw.

Timber-framed
A building whose skeleton is made from timber.

Travertine
A hard-wearing volcanic limestone.

Tree-nail
A wooden peg used to hold timber together in a timber-framed building.

Ziggurat
A high tower built in stepped stages with a temple at the top.

Super Structures Facts

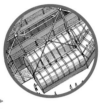

In the past 800 years the 180 ft (55 m) tall Leaning Tower of Pisa has tilted so much that the top now overhangs the bottom by about 16 ft (5 m).

The Seikan Tunnel, Japan, was built between 1971–1988. The greatest depth it reaches is 787 ft (240 m) under the sea.

The underground carpark of the Louisiana Superdome has spaces for 5,000 cars.

The Sydney Harbour Bridge, Australia, carries four railway lines and a road. When it was finished, 72 locomotives weighing a total of 7,600 tons drove over it. This was to test that it would be strong enough to support the weight of the traffic it was built for.

Each hour about 2,000 cars drive along St. Gotthard Tunnel's two-lane road in Switzerland. A new tunnel for trains is planned for completion in 2008. It will be 35 mi (57 km) long — the world's longest rail tunnel.

The Channel Tunnel lies, on average, 131 ft (40 m) beneath the seabed. Only about 125 ft (38 km) of the tunnel is under the sea — the rest is under dry land on either side of the Channel. It is the world's second longest rail tunnel.

The dome of the U.S. Capitol, Washington D.C., is 295 ft (90 m) high and about 98 ft (30 m) across.

The Motherland Statue, Russia, is made from reinforced concrete. In her right hand she holds a stainless steel sword, 89 ft (27 m) long and weighing 14 tons. This war memorial commemorates a World War II battle in which Russian forces defeated the invading German army.

The Shandaken Tunnel in New York City was the longest tunnel in the world when it was completed in 1924.

In the 1960s the temple of Ramesses II at Abu Simbel, Egypt, was saved from flooding. It was cut into huge blocks and rebuilt on higher ground.

Named after its architect, Gustave Eiffel, the Eiffel Tower was built for an exhibition and was only supposed to stand for 20 years.

Himeji Castle, Japan, is also called Shirasagi-jo, meaning White Heron Castle, because its top levels look like herons flying with their wings wide open.

Made from 1,500 tons of steel, the Millennium Wheel, London, England, has 80 spokes and 4 mi (6 km) of wire cable. It turns at 1.6 mph (2.5 kph) — slow enough for passengers to board its 32 French-made capsules without it having to stop.

A quick way to reach the CN Tower's Skypod, Toronto, Canada, its seven-story-high observation deck, is by elevator. In less than a minute visitors are whisked 1,152 ft (351 m) skywards.

More than 100,000 tons of steel and 80,780 mi (130,000 km) of wire cable were used in the construction of the Golden Gate Bridge, San Francisco. The suspension cables that hold the deck up are each 37 in (93 cm) in diameter formed from 27,572 separate strands of wire.

The Statue of Liberty was shipped across the Atlantic Ocean to New York in pieces. It is made from 300 thin sheets of copper, held together by rivets over an iron frame.

The Petronas Towers, Malaysia, is expected to lose its world record in 2001, when the 1,509-ft (460-m)-tall World Finance Center in Shanghai, China, is completed.

Each dome, or cupola, of St. Basil's Cathedral, Moscow, is made from pine. Painted wooden tiles, called shingles, are fastened onto them.

The Geodesic Golfball in Florida is an eighteen-story-high metal globe that contains a ride taking visitors on a journey through 10,000 years of human history.

The Great Pyramid and the Pharos of Alexandria in Egypt are two of the seven wonders of the ancient world.

It took 240,000 tons of travertine to build the Colosseum in Rome, Italy. The stone was brought from the quarries 12 mi (20 km) east of the city by barge and oxcart.

Index

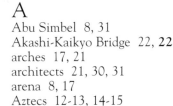